DROPPING IN ON Picasso

By Pamela Geiger Stephens
Illustrations by Jim McNeill

CrystalProductions
Aspen, Colorado   Glenview, Illinois

Library of Congress Cataloging-in-Publication Data

Stephens, Pamela Geiger.
  Dropping in on Picasso / written by Pamela Geiger Stephens;
  illustrated by Jim McNeill.— 1st ed.
      p. cm.
  ISBN 1-56290-325-X
  1. Picasso, Pablo, 1881-1973—Juvenile literature. 2. Art, Modern—
  20th century—Juvenile literature. I. McNeill, Jim, 1967- ill. II. Title.
  ND553.P5S79 2004
  709'.2—dc22
                                        2004022981

ISBN 1-56290-325-X

Printed in Hong Kong

Hello, there! My name is Puffer and I am on my way to the south of France to visit with the famous Spanish artist, Pablo Picasso. Mister Picasso lives in a small village near the Mediterranean Sea.

"Hello! How's the soup?"

Sluurpppp!

Puffer politely tips his hat, loses his balance, and falls from the sky.

W
  H
    O
      A
        A
          A
            A

Flap! Flap! Flap! Flutter! Flutter! Flap!

"Watch out! Heads up! Look out below!!"

Thump! Crash! Clang!

"What's that noise on my lawn?!" Mister Picasso asks.

Puffer has crash-landed onto Mister Picasso's bicycle. Pieces of the broken bicycle are on Puffer's head as he peeks into Mister Picasso's studio window.

"Hello, Mister Picasso! I am Puffer. You were expecting me, sir."

"Puffer! Oh, yes, the interviewer who is coming to see my artwork," Mister Picasso replies. "I wasn't expecting you to fall from the sky or to be so noisy!

"Please, dust yourself off and come into my studio," invites Mister Picasso.

"Thank you, that would be splendid!"

"I am very sorry about crashing into your bicycle, Mister Picasso."

"Not to worry! I can easily put it back together again," Mr. Picasso responds as he looks at the bicycle parts in his hands.

Then Mister Picasso asks, "I suppose that you are ready to learn about my life and artwork?"

"I am ready."

"Good!" exclaims Mister Picasso. "Let's start by looking at some photographs."

Mister Picasso opens a photograph album, points to a picture, and begins to tell about his life.

"I was born in Málaga, Spain.

"My father was an art teacher there. Maybe that is one reason why I became such a good artist," suggests Mister Picasso.

"Art was always my favorite subject in school. I drew and drew and drew. Sometimes I drew when I should have been doing something else," Mister Picasso laughs.

"When I was about thirteen years old, my father asked me to help him finish a painting.

"My job was to paint the feet of some pigeons.

"After I finished the painting, my father knew that I was becoming a fine artist," Mister Picasso says proudly. "My parents soon sent me to art school.

"I was such a good artist that my teachers said that I could skip the beginner classes if I could pass a very difficult art test," explains Mister Picasso. "I was given *only* one month to finish the test.

"But I did not finish the test in one month...

...I finished the test in one day!"
Mister Picasso chuckles.

"As I grew older, I began to visit art museums where I copied famous works of art.

"Soon I knew that to become a famous artist I had to move to Paris, France.

"Paris is where many modern artists lived and worked," says Mister Picasso as he shuts the photograph album.

Mister Picasso sighs and continues to tell Puffer his story.

"I was a very young man when I first moved to Paris. I was lonely and didn't have much money. My mood was sad most of the time. It seemed that wherever I looked, other people were sad, too.

"Because I was so unhappy, my paintings were unhappy, too. My artwork showed people like me who were alone and very sad. To show these ideas, I mainly used cool colors, especially blue. I used so much blue paint during this time that it is called my Blue Period," Mister Picasso says.

"When I became happier, the Blue Period came to an end. After that, I began to paint with warm colors. Would you like to see a warm color painting now?" asks Mister Picasso.

"Yes, please! I would like that very much."

"The title of this painting is *Family of Saltimbanques*," says Mister Picasso. "This time in my life is called the Rose Period because I used so many warm colors such as red and beige in my paintings.

"The warm colors show a different kind of mood than cool colors. If you look at the people and the place in the painting you will see what I mean.

"The people are circus performers who travel from town to town," Mister Picasso adds.

"But, Mister Picasso, if these people are circus performers, where are the colorful circus tents?"

"If I showed the circus tents, you would think about the fun of seeing a circus. By showing the people in an empty space, you get the idea that they feel as if they do not belong here. The warm colors add to this idea," replies Mister Picasso.

"Do you know that some people think that the painting is not about circus performers at all? It has been said that I am the man who is dressed in blue and that the other people are my artist friends," Mister Picasso hints.

"This is what makes art so interesting! The same painting can mean different things to different people."

"Exactly!" exclaims Mister Picasso. "Now let's look at an art style that I helped to invent."

"This is a painting that I call *Factory at Horta de Ebro*. The style of this painting is called Cubism," says Mister Picasso as he shows a painting of buildings and trees. "I helped to invent this style of art."

"What is Cubism, Mister Picasso?"

"Cubism is a kind of modern art that does not copy nature," Mister Picasso answers. "Everything in the picture is made from geometric shapes. There are not many details or colors.

"If you tell me what you see in this picture, perhaps that will better explain Cubism," Mister Picasso suggests.

"The picture seems very flat. I think this is because there are not many details or colors. And look! It is difficult to see where one building stops and another one starts. It is almost as if I can see all sides of one building at the same time!"

"That sometimes happens in Cubism," Mister Picasso explains. "Now let's look at another kind of Cubism that uses brighter colors."

"That would be splendid!"

"This painting is titled *Three Musicians*. What do you see that is different about this kind of Cubism?" asks Mister Picasso.

"The colors are much brighter and almost every object in the painting is made from triangles, rectangles, and polygons. The brightly colored shapes look almost as if you have cut them out and glued them onto the painting."

"Excellent!" Mister Picasso exclaims. "Do you see the three musicians?"

"Yes, I do! All three of them are facing us. The first is dressed in white. The second is dressed in red and yellow. And the third is dressed in black. Their clothes are very strange, Mister Picasso."

"That is because the musicians in this painting are actors who are wearing costumes and masks," Mister Picasso explains.

"Now look at the feet and hands of the musicians," directs Mister Picasso. "Do they look real?"

"The feet are just little boxes and the hands are much too small, but everything seems to fit together just right," says Puffer.

"Sometimes the objects in my paintings do not look real, but I always follow the rules for making good art," Mister Picasso adds. "Let's look at a portrait that I painted and you will see what I mean."

"I call this painting *Portrait of Dora Maar*," begins Mister Picasso.

"What a curious painting, Mister Picasso!"

"What? Why do you say that it is curious?" Mister Picasso asks.

"Look at Dora Maar's face. She is looking in two directions at the same time. Her skin is yellow and green and each of her eyes is a different color."

"Remember, my artwork does not always copy nature," says Mister Picasso. "But it does follow art rules. Look closely and you will see that the shapes and colors in the painting fit perfectly together.

"Imagine a line down the middle of the painting," Mister Picasso says. "Do you see how the shapes and colors are repeated on each side of the picture? This makes the portrait balanced. Balance is an art rule that I have followed in this painting.

"The shapes and colors also lead our eyes around the picture so that we are always looking at Dora Maar," continues Mister Picasso.

"I think I understand, Mister Picasso. Artists must follow art rules, but they do not have to copy nature."

"When artists do not copy nature, their artwork is sometimes called abstract."

"Abstract? What is abstract art, Mister Picasso?"

"Abstract art is a kind of modern art. Good abstract art follows the rules of art making, but it also shows new ideas about art.

"Cubism is just one kind of abstract art, like you saw in some of the paintings I showed you this afternoon.

"Here, Puffer, take these sheets of paper and draw yourself using two different ways of making abstract art."

Remembering what Mr. Picasso taught him, it doesn't take Puffer long to create two drawings.

"Mister Picasso, look at my drawings! I think I understand what you have been telling me.

"Those are very good drawings, Puffer. The color and shapes do not copy nature, and there are not many details. Now you have a hint about what abstract art can be."

As Mister Picasso and Puffer continue to talk about modern art, Puffer remembers another famous artist who lived and worked in Paris.

"Mister Picasso, when you lived in Paris, did you know the famous French artist, Henri Matisse?"

"Oh, yes! When Henri and I first met, we did not like each other's artwork very much," says Mister Picasso. "Later we became good friends.

"Now I think that Henri Matisse's artwork is the only art that is as good as mine!

"Henri and I have both used our studios as subjects for our paintings. Here, let me show you a painting of my studio," offers Mister Picasso.

"That would be terrific!"

"I call this painting *The Studio at Le Californie.* It was created here in this very place," says Mister Picasso.

"Some people think that this is more than a painting about my studio. It has been said that this is another of my self-portraits," Mister Picasso adds.

"A self-portrait? How could that be? This isn't a picture of you, Mister Picasso."

"You are right. I have not painted a picture of Picasso, but I have painted *ideas* about Picasso."

Then Mister Picasso explains, "The objects in the painting tell about me. You can see where I work, what I like, and how I felt when the painting was made."

"That must be why you show two paintings on the floor and a blank painting on the easel. An artist would always have artwork and materials in the studio."

"You are right! Anyone who sees this painting gets a peek inside of my studio, but they also learn a little about Pablo Picasso, the world-famous artist!" boasts Mister Picasso.

Mister Picasso picks up a newspaper and grumbles, "Where is that photograph?"

"Could I help you find something in the newspaper, Mister Picasso?"

"I want you to see a photograph of a sculpture that I designed for the city of Chicago," Mister Picasso replies. "It's in the newspaper somewhere!"

"When did you go to Chicago to make a sculpture, Mister Picasso?"

"I have never been to the United States," Mister Picasso answers when he finds the photograph in the newspaper.

"I don't understand. How could you create a sculpture for a place you've never been?"

"Let's look at the newspaper photograph and I'll try to explain," says Mister Picasso.

★ EXTRA! ★ EXTRA! ★ EXTRA! ★

PICASSO GIVES SCULPTURE TO CHICAGO!

The Chicago Picasso

"This is the sculpture that became known as the *Chicago Picasso*," Mister Picasso begins. "I never gave the sculpture a title.

"When I started this art project, I first drew my ideas about the sculpture and then made a small model in my studio. The model is about 42 inches tall. The finished sculpture is almost 50 feet tall and it weighs about 162 tons," says Mister Picasso.

"My goodness! How could such a big sculpture be made?"

"Many people in the United States worked together to copy the little model and make it larger," Mister Picasso replies and then proudly adds, "The sculpture was my gift to the city of Chicago."

"What a wonderful gift, Mister Picasso! Could you tell me what the sculpture is about?"

"Some people see a woman with long hair. Other people see a dog. Still other people see a cow's head. You can decide what you want to see. I never gave any hints about what it is," Mister Picasso answers.

"And that is what makes looking at art so much fun. There can be all sorts of right answers!"

An unusual clock hangs on the wall in Mister Picasso's studio. The clock suddenly makes a loud noise.

Gong!! Gong!! Gong!! Bang!! Brinnnggg!!

"I am not quite sure, Mister Picasso, but I think it might be time for me to go now."

"Good-bye, Mister Picasso. Thank you for sharing your artwork today."

Mister Picasso waves good-bye to Puffer. "Adiós, mi amigo! Good-bye, my friend. I hope to see you again soon."

"And here I go!"

Flap! Flap! Flap! Flutter! Flutter! Flap!

I hope you enjoyed dropping in on Pablo Picasso and finding out a little about his life and art. When we learn about artists and their art, we also learn about different times and places and ideas. The next time you visit an art museum, look for an artwork by Pablo Picasso. See if you can decide what the artwork is trying to say.

Until next time … adiós! Good-bye!

GLOSSARY

Abstract Art Artwork that is usually created through simplification or exaggeration of objects

Blue Period An early stage of Picasso's art career when his sadness showed in paintings created with a palette almost entirely of blue; Blue Period figures are usually elongated, without strong detail, and in deep thought

Cool Colors Generally blues and greens; colors that suggest cool temperatures as well as moods of sadness or calm; cool colors tend to recede on the picture plane

Cubism A type of modern art developed by Picasso and Georges Braque, Cubism had three phases: facet, analytic, and synthetic; objects in cubism are disassembled and then put back together in an abstract way

Rose Period A stage of Picasso's art career that followed the Blue Period; paintings developed a warm tone; characteristics of the subject matter include some ideas of isolation and unstable relationships

Matisse, Henri (1869-1954) One of the most important French artists of the twentieth century; best known as a father of Fauvism and later for his invention of paper cut-outs

Modern Art Art that breaks from the traditional style to explore new media, methods, processes, techniques, and ways of interpreting; generally considered to occur from the late nineteenth century throughout much of the twentieth century

Warm Colors Generally reds, oranges, and earth tones; colors that suggest warmth as well as a mood of excitement; warm colors tend to advance on the picture plane

Family of Saltimbanques, 1905. Oil on canvas, 83¾ x 90⅜ in. (2.128 x 2.296 cm). Chester Dale Collection. ©2004 Board of Trustees, National Gallery of Art, Washington, DC ©2004 Estate of Pablo Picasso/Artists Rights Society (ARS), New York

Factory at Horta de Ebro, 1909. Oil on canvas, 21 x 25 in. (53 x 64 cm). Hermitage, St. Petersburg, Russia Photo Credit: Erich Lessing/Art Resource, NY, ©2004 Estate of Pablo Picasso/Artists Rights Society (ARS), New York

Three Musicians, 1921. Oil on canvas, 79 in. x 87¾ in. Mrs. Simon Guggenheim Fund, ©The Museum of Modern Art, New York, NY. Licensed by SCALA/Art Resource, NY ©2004 Estate of Pablo Picasso/Artists Rights Society (ARS), New York

Portrait of Dora Maar, 1937. Oil on canvas, 33 x 25 in. (92 x 65 cm). Musée Picasso, Paris, France. Photo Credit: Réunion des Musées Nationaux/Art Resource, NY ©2004 Estate of Pablo Picasso/Artists Rights Society (ARS), New York

The Studio at Le Californie, 30 March 1956. Oil on canvas, 44½ x 57 in. (114 x 146 cm). Musée Picasso, Paris France Photo: J. G. Berizzi. Réunion des Musée Nationaux/Art Resource, NY ©2004 Estate of Pablo Picasso/Artists Rights Society (ARS), New York

Untitled Sculpture: Civic Center, Chicago Illinois Corten Steel, 50 ft. tall, 162 tons. Photo by Jennifer Treichler ©2004 Estate of Pablo Picasso/Artists Rights Society (ARS), New York